CW00422517

IAN BRODIE'S
NEW ZEALAND

ONE MAN'S LOVE AFFAIR
WITH HIS COUNTRY

HarperCollins*Publishers*

National Library of New Zealand Cataloguing-in-Publication Data
Brodie, Ian, 1957-
Ian Brodie's New Zealand / Ian Brodie.
ISBN 978-1-86950-696-4
1. New Zealand—Pictorial works. 2. New Zealand—Description
and travel. I. Title.
919.300222—dc 22

First published 2008
HarperCollins*Publishers (New Zealand) Limited*
P.O. Box 1, Shortland Street, Auckland

Copyright © Brodie Trust Limited 2008

Ian Brodie asserts the moral right to be identified as the author of this work.

All rights reserved. No part of this publication may be reproduced, stored in
a retrieval system or transmitted in any form or by any means, electronic,
mechanical, photocopying, recording or otherwise, without the prior written
permission of the publishers.

ISBN 978 1 86950 696 4

Cover design by Natalie Winter, HarperCollins Design Studio
Typesetting by IslandBridge

Printed and bound in China by Phoenix Offset Printing on 140gsm Matt Art

Introduction

Photos in translation

I was a lucky child because from an early age I was taken on holidays. Every summer after the rush of Christmas week, the car was packed and off we went on an adventure. Usually my favourite uncle and aunt came too and it was that happiness that close-knit families have along with the mutual enjoyment of exploration that made the times and places so special. They created lifelong memories as we visited Hawke's Bay, Taranaki, Tongariro, Tolaga Bay and on from Kaitaia to Bluff, places that opened my child's eyes to the beauty of our country.

For as long as I can remember, my dad and uncle had cameras. It seemed like every few minutes the car would stop and they would be out, changing lenses, discussing apertures and shutter speeds and climbing over fences to get that perfect shot.

When I was seven I was given an Instamatic camera for Christmas. As we packed the car and headed for the first time to New Plymouth, I was ecstatic. I too could take part in this ritual of stopping and discussing. The image of Mt Taranaki in this book is my homage to that journey; seeing that mountain for the first time is ingrained in my mind.

When I was twelve I visited the South Island and really fell in love: mountains, lakes, golden trees — we sometimes took five hours to travel 50 km but oh, the pictures we all made.

As I grew and had a family, my cameras were trusty companions. I loved landscapes and sometimes had to remember that we had gone to the lake to photograph the children, not the sunset against the schist.

This book is my translation of the places I love, memories from my childhood, memories of travelling with my children, places old and new, and my mind's translation into what they represent to me. It is unashamedly my perspective of our land.

I cherish each of the places in this book and they have been chosen because they reflect my passions, my interests, things that make this country special, from Second World War aeroplanes to flowers, beaches, mountains, Pinot Noir, cemeteries and film. Maybe I need to explain this a little further.

As a child I had one goal in my life: to be a pilot. This never happened but my love of the air remains. As the director of the New Zealand Fighter Pilots Museum I am very fortunate to have been able to sit in the open door of an aeroplane within ten metres of a thundering Merlin engine in a Mustang, moving like a ship in the invisible sea of air. Doubly special is the landscape underneath, making a joyous combination, one that I love to record. Then as a teenager I was going to be a film cameraman, filming our places. I first saw Roger Donaldson's film *Sleeping Dogs* when I was seventeen and that confirmed my chosen vocation.

Then, a part-time job in a travel agency to save for university sealed my fate to twenty years in that industry. Now I have gone full circle and am in that wonderful situation where all these early dreams and aspirations have combined.

When I return from travel, my garden is my true haven. I savour the perfection of nature and the way a flower can provide a fleeting love and sense of happiness. On a Saturday evening in the warmth of a Central Otago summer, the aroma of my garden competes with that special smell of a Central Pinot Noir. As I sit on my deck my mind takes me to places I have been. Some are well known, others are tucked away and are those wonderful moments you just happen to chance upon, a scene you will never forget. A perfect example of this is the buttercups on the West Coast. I went to explore a waterfall and came back with an image of something totally unexpected.

Ian Brodie's New Zealand is a celebration of my loves and memories of place. This book is dedicated to my family — Dianne, Travis, Sally-Anne and Belinda — and to the memory of my parents, to whom I am eternally grateful for starting my journey. This is for them, a translation of my love of my family into memories.

Ian Brodie, MNZM
Wanaka
May 2008

Poolburn sits high above Ophir and is in one of the more remote parts of Central Otago. If you want to fish, walk, 4WD or just enjoy the solitude, this is a wonderful place to visit. Made famous by *The Lord of the Rings* movie trilogy, it is a place that I return to over and over again. Each season creates dramatic differences in the landscape as it bakes in summer and freezes in winter, but there is always golden tussock and a distant snow-line.

When the makers of *The Lord of the Rings* decided to place Saruman's Isengard at the head of Lake Wakatipu, I could not have agreed with them more. As one stands here and looks west towards the Southern Alps you can certainly believe you are looking at the Wizard's Vale. Tolkien's descriptive text matches this view perfectly.

Opposite and right The slender Dorothy Falls are a gem in the bush near Lake Kaniere on the West Coast. The loop road from Hokitika that takes you to these falls circuits the lake to Kowhitirangi before returning to town. Numerous scenic gems cajole you to stop, and really a full day is needed to enjoy the pristine bush, beautiful lake and falls. As you park near the falls, take a walk in the opposite direction towards the lake. I have wandered this path many times, and always the sheer greenness of the place holds me mesmerised as I meander along.

Left The tactical importance of North Head was soon realised when the first Europeans arrived in Auckland. During the 1870s there was a totally unfounded fear that the Russians were planning to attack our ports, and thus began the strategic history of this headland. Over the next hundred years the area was an important naval base and the site of the main gun emplacements protecting the harbour. In 1976 the navy departed and the area is now administered by the Department of Conservation as a public reserve.

Below left The harbourside suburb of Devonport is arguably one of the best Auckland suburbs in which to live. A shopping centre provides all the necessities and the city centre is only minutes away by ferry. The opening of the Auckland Harbour Bridge in 1959 eased the water traffic, but now has its own bottleneck because of the huge increase in motor traffic caused by the Auckland population boom. Devonport remains an oasis in this traffic explosion, and the fine Victorian houses combined with its nearness to the city make it my favourite part of Auckland. I remember standing here with my father looking at this vista, which has changed very little in the foreground but dramatically so in the background.

Below right John Ballance looks out on Wellington from in front of the Parliamentary Library. Although most of us complain about the activities of our MPs with monotonous regularity, this should not stop us visiting the seat of power. The library was designed by Thomas Turnbull in the Victorian Gothic style and partially opened in 1883. The main building (centre) has a slightly younger pedigree; it opened in 1907 to replace the previous building that was destroyed by fire. The Beehive, as it is known to all New Zealanders, was first planned by Sir Basil Spence, a British architect, who designed the concept during a visit to Wellington in 1964. It was not completely finished until 1979.

Above left   Clouds reflect white rock formations near Kaikoura.

Above right   In one direction, the calm sea, and in the opposite direction, the amazing colours of the sun as it farewells the day.

Left   Sunset, Kaikoura.

Above left   I consider any time spent on a film set a privilege — one that very few people get to enjoy. To be able to work freely to photograph the cast and crew as they attend to their work is very special. Here the director of photography Don McAlpine (left) and director Andrew Adamson develop a scene for *The Lion, the Witch and the Wardrobe* at Elephant Rocks near Duntroon in the Waitaki Valley.

Above right   Andrew Adamson and Tilda Swinton discuss the script.

Opposite above   The road between Christchurch and Arthur's Pass is one of contrasts. The flat Canterbury Plains give way to the Southern Alps in a dramatic change of altitude before levelling off to a meandering drive with mountains on all sides. In 2004 the normally brown tussock at Castle Hill changed dramatically to a verdant spread of rich green. It was here that the final battle scene in *The Lion, the Witch and the Wardrobe* was filmed, and spring green was a necessity. A year of sowing produced this beautiful result. Filming was undertaken here in December, but then one morning, as if by the power of the White Witch to prove her reign was not over, snow appeared. The resultant scene of green and snow will probably never be repeated.

Left and opposite below   Another huge attraction when visiting film sets is the opportunity to visit parts of New Zealand you probably never knew about. I had travelled the Arthur's Pass route between Christchurch and Greymouth often, and Castle Rocks was always a place to visit another time. Now it had become the scene of the Great Battle at the end of *The Lion, the Witch and the Wardrobe* and my journey was stopping here. The expanse of plain is a natural amphitheatre set against the Southern Alps. Surrounded by seemingly impenetrable mountains, this area looks exactly as C.S. Lewis described it. An ample supply of irrigation provided the green grass, which looked implausible given the brown surroundings.

Above Following the massacre that was the First World War, every town or village in the Commonwealth erected monuments to the 'glorious dead'. Their sacrifice should never be forgotten, but I do wonder how many visitors to Picton cast their eyes up at this memorial and give thanks to these young men who gave the ultimate in a land far removed from their home.

Right Our New Zealand fighter pilots saw service in every theatre of the Second World War. Sadly, they died there as well, so very few of these chaps are actually buried in New Zealand. One is Sergeant John Aperehama Tirikatene, who now lies in the Kaiapoi (Old North Road) Maori Cemetery.

Left   The beautiful green of New Zealand flax near Lake Tarawera.

Above   The gnarled trunk of a pohutukawa at Scott Point on the Mahurangi Peninsula, north of Auckland.

Opposite   During our teenage travels in a Kombi, the jewel in our crown was the coast over Blackjack Hill at Opito Bay on the Coromandel Peninsula. This wonderful sandy beach saw many midnight barbecues, and during the many weekends spent in this idyllic place we hardly ever saw another soul. Returning just a few years back the beach looked exactly the same, but now a number of baches have been built to enjoy the view. Can you blame anyone for doing this? Not at all, but to me the isolation of 35 years ago was a better memory.

Left Thirty years ago, if a local had said there would be cranes building high-rise apartments in Queenstown by 2000, he would have been laughed out of town. The rate at which this small alpine town has grown in that 30-year period has been phenomenal. Now known as the adventure capital of New Zealand, Queenstown receives over 1.3 million visitors annually from around the world. If you want to raise your adrenaline, this is the town to come to, and the spectacular scenery is still a major reason to visit.

Above The promise of vintages to come is borne on the leaves of these grapevines at Nevis Bluff Vineyard in the Gibbston Valley. The results are always consistent — one of the best pinot noir in the world.

Right   Cable Bay may seem an unusual name for a Northland beach. This place marks the spot where the telephone cable finally arrived from Queensland in 1902 and at that time it was the longest single cable in the world. The bay is a place of baches, golden sands and the never-ending murmur of surf that lulls even the worst insomniac into a gentle sleep.

Below left   One of the best seafood restaurants in Southland is situated near Riverton, but this is just one reason to take the 45-minute drive from Invercargill. Here, the climate is good, the seafood is abundant, the beaches feature wonderful rock pools to scramble over, and the harbour always looks resplendent with the fishing smacks sitting gracefully in the estuary. The town lays claim to being the oldest in Southland and Otago, and indeed has had a population since 1821 when whalers first moved to the area. The hardship of this life gave way in the late 1800s, but Riverton still has many links to the sea, and serves as a community centre for the rich green surrounding farmlands.

Below right   Driftwood on the beach near Opotiki. The beaches here are a Mecca for sun-lovers every summer, and the annual exodus from cities for the Christmas break is particularly evident.

Above   This miner's cottage beside the main road from Queenstown to Cromwell looks idyllic in 2007, but spare a thought for the original inhabitants of 150 years ago. The Central Otago region of the 1800s was one of hardship, as settlers battled with the extreme temperatures, remoteness and even a little lawlessness. The cottage is built from stacked stone in a manner similar to that used by the many Scottish immigrants in their homeland.

Left   I believe the Kiwi farm shed deserves a patent. That great combination of iron sheets and whatever wood is to hand has been the mainstay of our rural community for over 200 years. The sheds can store so many amazing objects that one day they will be an archaeologist's dream. Whenever I see a shed like this (near Owaka in the Catlins) I want to climb the fence and peer in. A 1936 Chevrolet may be sitting quietly inside, forgotten by all, just crying out to be tidied up so that once again she may purr down the gravel roads as she used to.

Opposite   The Early Settlers Museum at Greytown. Greytown was first settled in 1854, and its wonderfully restored cottages and trees provide a welcome antithesis for Wellingtonians who travel over the Rimutakas and escape the city for an afternoon of antiques and good food. The first Arbour Day celebration in New Zealand was held here in 1890, and the town's love of trees must surely stem from this and the work of inspired locals. One I particularly admire is Stella Bull who has a park bench dedicated to her with a plaque with her own words: *'Only God can make a tree'.* The town boasts the most complete street of Victorian architecture in the country.

THIS COTTAGE IS ONE
OF THE FIRST ERECTED
IN GREYTOWN BY
MR TOWERSEY (

Travelling between Queenstown and Te Anau, there are many diversions
to places of splendour which only a few tourists seem to take. From
Mossburn a drive on loose metal through brown hills will take you to some
of the most pristine lakes of Southland. Mavora Lakes sit on the fringe
of grassland and bush, presenting a mixture of gold and green for the
photographer. Here the nor'west wind and resultant cloud often create a
shaded canopy over the beech and distant tussock, but the two seem to
have a symbiotic relationship, each knowing the other's boundaries.

The Fiordland area can receive more rain in a day than Blenheim does
in a month. This can be frustrating for those on a quick visit, but I am
lucky enough to be able to visit when the weather suits. I do like the rain
and mist though — they add another dimension of mood to an already
charged atmosphere. As the mist swirls around the peaks surrounding
Lake Manapouri, I relish the mystique of hidden peaks, dark forest and
occasional glimpses of the sun that lightens the clouds.

A saltworks is an intriguing place and as a lover of salt I just had to visit. Lake Grassmere is situated south of Blenheim with sand dunes separating the lake from the sea. A strong northwesterly prevailing wind and high temperatures make this the ideal location to produce salt. The lake is divided into solar evaporation ponds, and seawater is pumped in and moved between ponds over several months. The water increases in salinity with each successive evaporation period, and as salinity increases, crystallised salt forms and is extracted. Most of our salt comes from this single area, and at the end of summer when harvesting commences, the huge white mounds are a spectacular sight.

Somehow, the taste of most food here in New Zealand seems to surpass the best of any other country — it just tastes real. Strawberries are no exception. The red juiciness that falls from the fruit is a perfect counterpoint to the green stalks. Nothing says summer more than strawberries.

Central Otago produces the best pinot noir in the world, and from this amazing collection two varieties always vie for my attention. On one side is Nevis Bluff and on the other is Mt Difficulty. Even if you don't like wine, visit Mt Difficulty for the amazing counterpoint of rugged rocks and the green vines that cling to the slopes. I am a real fan of English chef Rick Stein and he visited Mt Difficulty recently to order wine for his restaurant in Padstow, Cornwall. That says a lot to me about its quality.

Opposite above Early morning mist swirls through the trees at Mt Nicholas Station. It may seem odd but I love the fog. The enveloping nature of this swirling dampness reminds me of prose from Keats and text from Tolkien. Maybe they felt the same!

Opposite below I had to title this picture 'Will You Dance With Me?' I was actually trying to capture the sunset at Kaikoura when I turned in the opposite direction. Like a virile male talking to a blushing maiden, these two trees caught my attention against the gathering gloom.

Right The road between Te Anau and Milford Sound is a much-frequented tourist track, with buses, cars and campervans travelling to view the famous Mitre Peak. I prefer the drive rather than the destination, where at every turn in the road a distant mountain appears, a stream busily wanders and the clouds play with the horizon. Not more than ten metres from this busy highway I sat for hours as the sun fought with the clouds over this one tree which was clothed in moss, rather like an Ent in *The Lord of the Rings*, and seemingly enjoying the struggle as much as I did.

Every year, many thousands of tourists make the trek to Cape Reinga, the northernmost point of New Zealand. Rightly so, but I wonder how many take the detour to Matai Bay on the Karikari Peninsula. With its wonderful curve of pure white sand, this harbour is the epitome of a tropical island. However, most Kiwis make the pilgrimage to tropical islands overseas, and who can blame them. A traveller from Christchurch (or any point south of about Rotorua in reality) can travel to the Gold Coast of Australia for much less than it costs to get here. Then again, maybe that is a good thing.

In my late teens my friends down the road bought a VW Kombi van — an old one that belched smoke and seemed to falter on every hill. However, this was our transport away from the city, and weekends were planned with great precision to leave the high-rises for something a little more 'pretty'. The Coromandel Peninsula was our escape and we roamed this region, enjoying the escape from the regime that wanted to control us (as teenagers do). A good dose of Pink Floyd and a ripped tarpaulin on the beach to sleep under were all we needed. Thirty years later I returned for the first time and nothing seemed to have changed. The Kombi was gone, but the memories lingered.

The autumn market on the Queenstown lakeshore provides an opportunity for local clothing designers to showcase their wares against an appropriate backdrop. The weather is normally calm, and with the sun providing her warming rays, an alfresco lunch is a delight.

Colourful hand-made cushions for sale in Seymour Square, Blenheim during the village fair at Hunter's Garden Marlborough.

Left above and below   The Whanganui River stretches 290 km from the northern slopes of Mt Tongariro in the Central Plateau to the sea at Wanganui. It is our longest navigable river and third longest overall. During the early 1900s the river was one of our major tourist attractions. As Wanganui grew as a settlement and trading post, the river became the main route to the interior, with a number of river boats plying its length with goods for sale to the locals. As the river's fame spread, inquisitive tourists also began to travel the lower reaches by boat, and the tourism industry in this region was born.

Below   Leaving Raetihi and travelling northwards you must make a detour to the Ruatiti Domain. If one imagines the ideal place to pitch a tent, this is it. In the middle of summer I can picture the idle holiday-maker lazing in the long grass beside the slow-flowing river, with maybe a newspaper or novel cast to one side as the sound of busy insects lulls them into a warm and cosy slumber. When it is time to eat, the river can provide the sustenance, and as the sun gives way to a warm twilight, smoke curls from the barbecue.

Left The Bertie Wooster era come alive in Napier. The debilitating earthquake in the region in 1931 destroyed almost all of the city's buildings which led to a total rebuild. Art deco was a very popular style at this time, and therefore most buildings here are created in that style. Napier must stand as one of the most complete art deco cities in the world, and the locals embrace this and are very proud of their heritage. Tours of the buildings attract many visitors, and the local car clubs join the style with appropriate vehicles and, of course, dress-ups. I love this town of wonderful buildings, friendly people and wonderful climate, and enjoy wandering the streets, drinking in the architecture.

Opposite above The façade of the Ellison & Duncan building in Napier. Originally destroyed in the 1931 earthquake, the building was designed by Napier architect J.A. Louis Hay as part of the reconstruction of Napier.

Opposite below I don't follow sport much, except for cricket, and maybe because right in my home village I have a place to watch it. The Luggate Cricket Ground plays host to many local matches over the summer. The vista of trees, the gurgling of the Luggate Creek and the hum of bees combine to create the perfect background to the thwack of leather on willow.

Left This image would have to rate in the harder category to capture. I like my creature comforts, and this night on the beach at Hokitika offered none. The roaring southerly wind blew the surf back in some form of defiance against nature, and I stood frozen to the spot, waiting for a brief glimpse of sun. The image may seem rather ordinary to most, but to me it will always conjure up bitterly cold fingers and total darkness as the sun slipped quietly away in this seemingly godforsaken part of the world.

Below left As I wandered this remote location near Denniston I came across a small house, destroyed by fire, and these remains nearby. Had some family decided to live at this lofty height, only to have their dreams shattered by the tragedy of flame? The surrounding hills remained covered in cloud and a misty rain fell on the scene — as if the land missed these pioneers as well and was still mourning the loss.

Below right The locality of Paradise is aptly named. Here the mountains tower around in all directions, and the native bush exudes that wonderful freshness that only seems to exist in this country. This part of New Zealand was relatively undiscovered until about five years ago. Now land prices have skyrocketed, and I can only wish that I had purchased my own piece of Paradise ten years ago.

Left Autumn and Arrowtown, in Central Otago, combine to create an enchantment only seen in this part of New Zealand. All senses are assailed. Early-morning frosts provide a crackle in the air which turns to warmth by lunchtime. Add to this the aromas of burning wood and damp leaves, and shake together with a clarity of sight and a silence that is only broken by the sigh of leaves that realise their summer is over. The historic mining cottages are now thankfully protected to allow images like this to continue to be taken in perpetuity.

Opposite above It might be electricity, but the fitting is perfect. Arrowtown in autumn provides such wonderful colour combinations — a palette perfected by nature.

Opposite below A restful place to sit on the shores of Lake Te Anau.

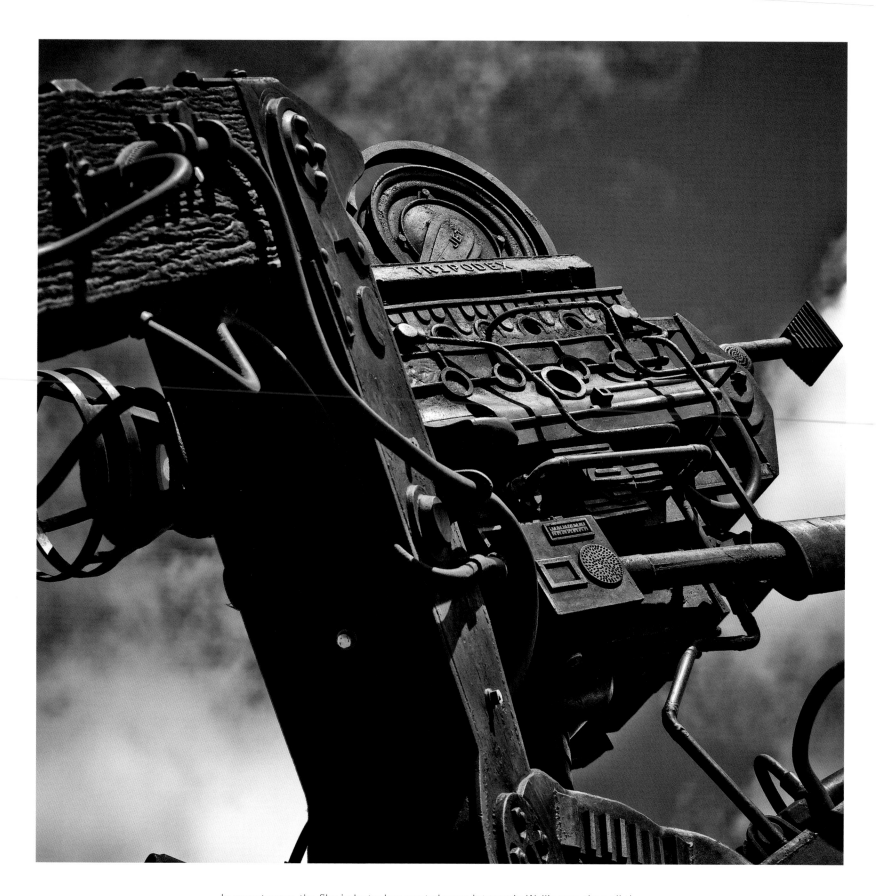

In recent years, the film industry has created more interest in Wellington than all the rhetoric from our parliamentarians. Colloquially known as 'Wellywood', this symbol of our burgeoning film industry takes pride of place on Courtenay Place, opposite the newly restored Embassy Theatre. Designed by the craftsmen of Weta Workshop, it is a constant reminder that we have come a long way in the last ten years.

My love of the sea (from a distance) stems from the evocative ending to *The Lord of the Rings* where Sam and his companions farewell part of the Fellowship and hear the sound of the sea as it comes ashore at the Grey Havens. Since reading that and listening to Bo Hansson's album inspired by *The Lord of the Rings*, I have often tried to capture the majesty of water. Here in Gisborne the sea rolls onto the shore in Middle-earth Aotearoa.

Left above   The Ratana Church at Raetihi is an icon of the area. I specifically wanted to capture the brightness of the church — its red and white colours are so vivid. Driving towards it on an overcast rainy day I was bitterly disappointed that my wish was probably not going to come true. A little closer to the scene, a single shaft of light appeared from the heavens and perfectly illuminated the colours. The hardest thing was to stop the car and capture this beauty before the sun hid behind the grey mantle again. I managed to take one photo and then it all turned dark, so thank you, whoever you may be, that watched over me this rainy day.

Left below and opposite   The Anglican church at Raukokore, in the far eastern Bay of Plenty, must be one of the most photographed in the country. Built in 1894 it originally had a large whale jawbone framing its entrance, but this has now been removed to the Whakatane Museum. It has stood the test of time remarkably well, considering its precarious position flanked by the sea on three sides. The sun-bleached headstones and white wood make a remarkable contrast to the blue sky, and provide empathy with the white cirrus cloud.

Morning cloud lies over Wellington Harbour looking north towards the Hutt Valley.

Invercargill boasts one of the best beaches for driving on in New Zealand. Oreti Beach stretches over 26 km, and one of the best ways to enjoy it is to take the 4WD and just drive away from civilisation. Another great thing about this beach is the sunset. Invariably there is a little cloud, and as the sun rushes to meet the sea a kaleidoscope of colour envelops your vision. If you visit here on the longest day, be prepared for a wait — situated so far south, the long twilight of a Southland evening means that night won't fall until well after 10.30 p.m.

I call this photo 'Waiting for the Fence to Break'. With frustration the cow appears to be looking at the nice new fence post that the farmer has put in to replace the one that has rotted away. The wind and rain on the West Coast are certainly hard on anything wooden, and I wonder how long the original post had stood there, keeping in the herd.

When I show this picture to people, many immediately say 'Scotland', and although this cottage, green hills and water may make this assumption plausible, in reality it is Deborah Bay near Port Chalmers. The early Scottish pioneers settled in this area, and with so many reminders of home, who can blame them?

Left above   *Rosa Loving Memory*, Wanaka Airport.

Left centre   *Rosa Faithful Friend*, Luggate.

Left below   *Rosa Kaikoura*, War Memorial Park, Kaikoura.

Above   Tulips in Queens Park, Invercargill.

Below   *Lonicera*, Barewood Gardens, Seddon.

Right above *Papaver rhoeas*, Luggate.

Right centre Nature creates perfect symmetry in this rock rose growing near the beach at Kaikoura.

Right below I had to include the stately *Alcea* (hollyhock). It was brought out to New Zealand by the first English settlers. I guess the plant reminded them of stately gardens and thatched cottages. The genus grows very well in this country and is a prolific producer of seeds, ensuring plenty of plants and colours each summer.

Butchers Dam is only 5 km from Alexandra in Central Otago. The dam was created to supply power to the district, and time has aged the area perfectly. There are several picnic spots and walking tracks in the vicinity, and it makes for a wonderful day trip from Wanaka. Situated 300 m above sea level, this lake is a grandstand for seasonal changes. This photo was taken on a warm spring afternoon when the temperature tipped 20°C. Three months earlier the entire area was clothed in a freezing hoar frost.

The small bay of Closeburn is a gem. As the road leaves Queenstown taking you towards Glenorchy, it drops down to this delightful bay where the calm waters of the lake lap serenely across the shingle. In summer there is a sweet smell in the air of native herbs and the gentle calling of birds. This would have to be one of the best barbecue spots in the world.

Opposite and above   I took great pleasure in capturing this scene. I wanted to photograph the sun as it set behind the Kaikoura Ranges and cast its light on the Pacific, and it just happened that the best place was opposite the Pier Hotel. As I waited for the sun to work its magic, the landlady enquired as to what I was doing with cameras and tripods. The answer gave almost instant gratification — we arranged to barter a good Marlborough wine and local mussels against a copy of the print.

Right   The colour of a sunset is reflected in the calm sea and off the small rocks opposite the Pier Hotel, Kaikoura.

Above and left Reminders of the great coal-mining days of Denniston linger in the discarded remnants of machinery. When staying in Westport, a trip to the abandoned Denniston Mine is a must. Situated 520 m above sea level, a rich coal seam was discovered in 1873. The major problem, however, was getting the coal down from this altitude to the waiting ships at Westport. An ingenious railway incline system was developed in 1879 and coal was successfully taken from this bleak plateau until 1967. Now all that remains are the remains — one of the best ghost towns in the world.

Above The Kawana Mill at Matahiwi on the Whanganui River dates back to the 1850s and was one of a series of initiatives by Governor Sir George Grey to encourage Maori to be self-sufficient. In August 1854 the Reverend Richard Taylor of the Church Missionary Society, the millwright (Peter McWilliam) and local Maori built the mill from totara logs salvaged from the Whanganui River. The cast-iron machinery and brass bearings were brought out from England. The millstones were imported from Australia and were a personal gift from Grey, thus the mill was named using a transliteration of its benefactor's name — Kawana Kerei.

Right I just had to stop at this old abandoned timber mill beside the main road to Whangaroa on my journey through the Far North. I have a fascination with old relics — maybe that's why I look after a museum — but more than that, it was the contradictory nature of the machinery that captured my interest. A hundred years ago this piece of equipment would have been the pride of a mill worker. It would have been oiled, maintained and providing for its master, but it now lies abandoned — rubbish from a bygone era whose only use is to provide idle amusement for a passing photographer.

Above The differing geographic nature of our two major islands is especially evident in the lush native bush and rolling hills that abound in the north. The walk to Dawson Falls on the slopes of Mt Taranaki is a delight. Within minutes of leaving the road, the well-formed path transports you into the most wonderful bush setting, with ancient trees mixing with the well-watered moss.

Opposite Mt Taranaki from Lake Mangamahoe. One of the first photos I ever made was taken at this same spot over 40 years ago. Between Instamatic and digital 16 megapixel there is a huge difference but the sense of mountain and lake remains the same as I saw it then.

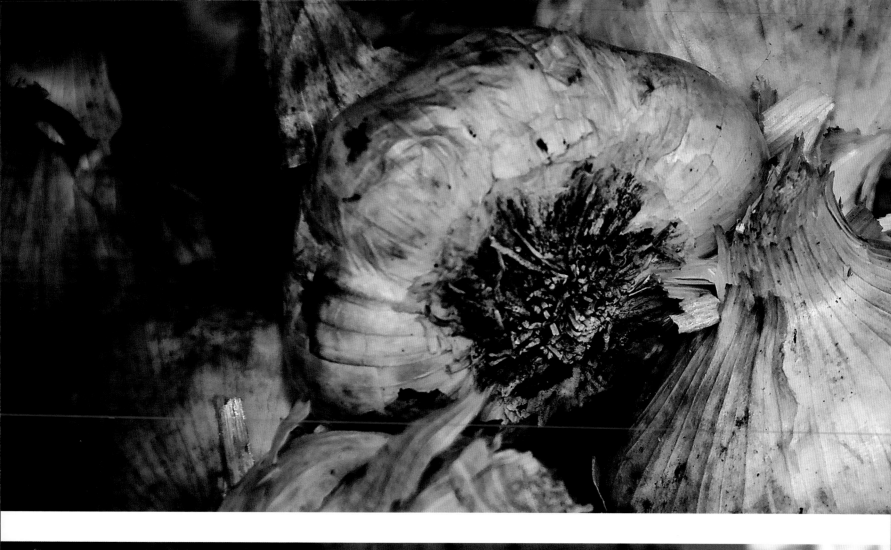

Beautiful smoked New Zealand garlic for sale at the
Hunter's Garden Marlborough festival.

A good English stilton or French brie is pretty hard to beat.
We have done it though — and in less than 30 years. It
feels like a long time ago that all that was available in
New Zealand was the 'cheese' called Chesdale.

I don't think I could live in a temperate zone where the only change in season is evidenced by a slight change in temperature. In Central Otago, spring is welcomed by longer days, lesser frosts and gathering winds, but most importantly by blossoms on the trees. Here at Clyde the trees start to wake up from their winter slumber and the orchardists commence their work, preparing for the summer harvest.

The combination of geography, weather events and altitude always provide a varied sky at home. A two-minute walk from the house one late-winter afternoon provided a wonderful view of an approaching cold front. The layers of sky to me work beautifully with the bare willows that seem to be hunkering down, waiting for the cold wind to arrive.

To obtain a true appreciation of Queenstown you need to visit it at least twice in all four seasons. Here it is early winter and a southerly has crept up from Kingston at the southern end of Lake Wakatipu to place the first tendrils of snow on The Remarkables. The brown tussock has disappeared under a white blanket, albeit briefly. A change to northerlies and warmth the next day could see the temperatures rise again to over 20°C. Despite the huge expansion of population in the Queenstown area, there are still many places where you could be a million miles from civilisation.

'Dragon Fish', Susan Holmes, Auckland, Supreme Award Winner, 1996 Montana WOW Awards

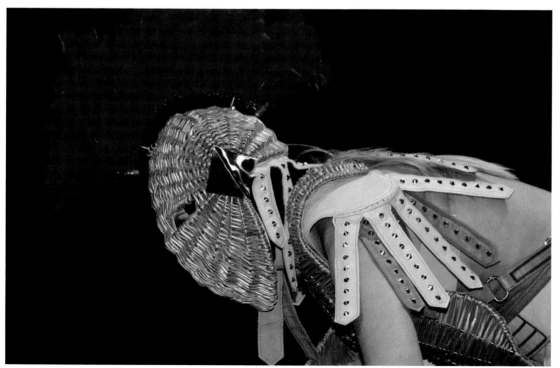

'The Guardian', Chris Flaherty, Nelson, American Express Open Section, 2007 Montana WOW Awards

I must say I am not a fan of indoor festivals and shows, and so the thought of attending the Montana World of WearableArt Awards Show in Wellington was slightly disagreeable to me. Dianne, my wife, is the opposite though, and last year I finally relented and we attended this annual showcase of design talent from around the world. All I can say is that prejudices are a terrible thing — from the moment the show started until the fantastic finale, I sat entranced. The colour, the effects, the choreography, the sheer artistic talent — it all captured me. If there is one show you must visit in New Zealand, it is this one.

American Express Open Section Dance Scene, 2007 Montana WOW Awards

'Te Ahua Whenua — Earth Forms', Wendy Burton and Patrick Duffy, Christchurch, Runner-up Air New Zealand South Pacific Section, 2007 Montana WOW Awards

CentrePort White Section Dance Scene, 2007 Montana WOW Awards

'Borderlines', Janet Bathgate, Nelson, Air New Zealand South Pacific Section, 2007 Montana WOW Awards

'Bi-psyche', Rita Schrieken and Phillipa Ruegg, Paraparaumu, American Express Open Section, 2007 Montana WOW Awards

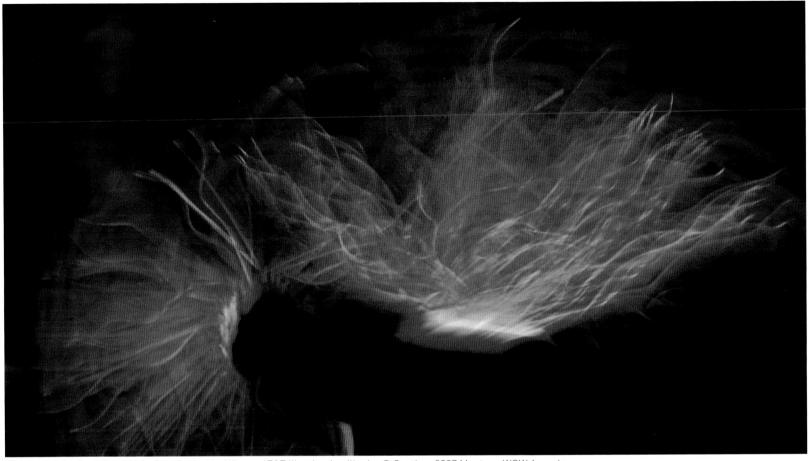

'Flowers of the Sea', Cheryl Linaker, Australia, Winner AT&T Illumination Illusion® Section, 2007 Montana WOW Awards

'Pallas Athene', Donna Demente, Oamaru, Montana Supreme Award Winner,
1991 Montana WOW Awards

'Puhiwahine — Maori Poetess', Te Waiata Hamm, Taumarunui, Air New Zealand
South Pacific Section, 2007 Montana WOW Awards

The Arts Centre in Christchurch within the stone buildings of the original University of
Canterbury is a series of eclectic shops selling a multitude of wares. How far-sighted
the planners were to allow these buildings to remain standing and use them in a way
that benefits locals and tourists alike. I can spend many hours here browsing for objects
I don't really need, but at the same time marvelling at the stone architecture that sets
this city apart from any other in New Zealand. It is as if the English settlers arrived here
and immediately transplanted their part of the world to make an antipodean version.
The modern statues combine so well with the existing architecture. I believe many cities
in the world could take a lesson from this inspired planning.

Left   The lake shore at Wanaka glistens in a wintry sun with a perfect backdrop of snow that would gladden the heart of any skier. Personally I would rather sit on the lakefront and enjoy this view rather than hurtle around on some planks.

Below left   The early winter of 2007 gave us a snow fall of over 10 cm. As the sun came out, there was an eerie silence created by the blanketing snow. The last remnants of autumn still showed on our cherry trees as the snow slowly melted.

Below right   High in the peaks around Mt Earnslaw the snow takes a long time to release its icy mantle. Even in late November the vestiges of winter remain, despite the sprouting of tussock and parahebe.

Left and above The Haast Pass route, between Haast and Lake Hawea, features a diverse landscape that teaches a lot about the orographic effect of mountains on rainfall. Leaving Haast, the road travels through dense bush as it skirts the Haast River. A steady climb then commences towards the 563 m summit. The picnic stop at Pleasant Flat lives up to its name – I always stop here to drink in the aroma of our native bush and sit beside the river that meanders across the shingle. The best is yet to come though, and at the Gates of Haast I always stop to marvel at nature and her beauty. A single-lane bridge that looks as if it should have been used in *Where Eagles Dare* crosses the thundering Haast River. The river is just a sideshow, though, to the huge rocks embedded in its path. Park the car and walk under the bridge to this vantage point – you will not be disappointed.

Above The fern has inspired generations of decorative artists. The *Silver Fern* was the name of the passenger railcar that ran from Auckland to Wellington between 1970 and 1991. Increasingly, there have been calls for the silver fern to replace the Union Jack on the New Zealand flag. Above all, it is the sense of pride associated with its place on sports jerseys and in the names of national teams, such as netball's Silver Ferns and rugby's Black Ferns (women) and the All Blacks (men), that gives the fern an unassailable place in New Zealand's culture.

Right The cabbage tree (*Cordyline australis*) grows abundantly throughout New Zealand, no matter what the climatic conditions are. On the West Coast they flourish in the most remote places where one wonders if there is any nourishment to be gained from the salt-laden sandy soil. During the 1800s the leaves of the plant were boiled up as a replacement for cabbage — hence the name. The tree bears no other resemblance to the vegetable.

Right The L-39 Albatros is a familiar sight above Wanaka. Designed in 1966, the Czechoslovakian trainer was a great success with the Soviet, Czech and East German air forces, among others. Now a popular warbird, the foreground example is owned by local pilot Robert Borrius-Broek. Its sleek shape is often seen in the area as Robert enjoys the aircraft's excellent performance and outstanding handling characteristics. I was very fortunate to obtain this image when Robert was joined by an example assembled in Wanaka for an Australian owner. It was flown across the Tasman two days later.

Below left and right Swede Mikael Carlsson is an enthusiast. Twice now he has visited Wanaka with his 1909 Bleriot and entertained the crowds at the three-day Warbirds Over Wanaka show. For me, Mikael is a link to the beginning of aviation in this country. Our first fighter pilot, Joseph Hammond, flew a Bleriot like this in 1914. Mikael is a gentleman who understands aviation heritage and gets the most pleasure out of sharing his knowledge. I like that a lot.

Opposite above The similarities between the Highlands of Scotland and Central Otago are numerous. Although the mountains may be on a bigger scale, a Scotsman would feel very much at home here. Many do, in fact, as they migrated here in their thousands. I was privileged to be able to photograph some of the sets of the major motion picture *The Water Horse* when principal photography was being undertaken on Lake Wakatipu. The addition of this wonderful Highlanders croft completed the scene and affirmed in my mind the similarities.

Opposite below The Anglican Cemetery in Lyttelton. This would have to be one of the eeriest cemeteries I have visited in New Zealand. The older graves are in a wonderful state of disrepair, and I can imagine it would be an interesting place to walk at night. New Zealand film director Peter Jackson thought so too and used this place extensively in his film *The Frighteners*.

Right above In 2006 an international film crew spent a month at Queenstown filming *The Water Horse*. Telling the story of the Loch Ness monster, the producers decided that the rugged landscape around Mt Nicholas worked as a perfect double for the highlands of Scotland. The weather gods played the game and on one of the first days of shooting a perfect sunrise captured the film crew on the shores of Lake Wakatipu.

Right below In 2003 the glitterati of Hollywood descended on Taranaki to film a major portion of *The Last Samurai*. It's easy to see why, even if you overlook the Mt Fuji-shaped Mt Taranaki. The western coasts of both the North and South Islands receive substantial rain from the Tasman-born fronts, giving a very green sheen to the countryside. North of New Plymouth, part of a farm was commandeered to create a small Japanese village in the late Samurai period. Most of the sets have gone, but this imposing torii gate remains.

Right Knights Point, situated north of Haast township on the rugged West Coast, is a wonderful seascape of jutting rocks, emerald sea and green tree-clad hills. It was at this place that the Haast Pass road was completed in 1965 and I always enjoy stopping here to admire the vista. Only a two-hour drive from land-locked Central Otago, this place is the epitome of the West Coast as the wild seas crash on the rocks far below and the senses are assailed by the aroma of damp bush.

Below left The Waitoto Valley reaches from the Southern Alps near Mt Aspiring down to the Tasman Sea on the West Coast. This waterfall is just one of hundreds that flow with spring snow melt. On the day I visited, the temperature was warm, the icy water provided a musical background, and all we needed was a barbecue and a nice glass of pinot to complete heaven on earth.

Below right Stones on a West Coast beach.

Right   The view from high on the Crown Range between Wanaka and Queenstown always takes my breath away. To the left is the Gibbston Valley Winery (one of the first vineyards in the region) whilst centre (in the shade) is the first commercial bungy jump site in the world. To the right is another pioneer winery, Chard Farm. The Gibbston Valley has recently picked up on the catch phrase 'valley of wines' and how appropriate this is. From the early days of the late 1970s when vineyard pioneer Alan Brady planted the first stock, this narrow valley has blossomed and now has over 20 vineyards producing quality wine.

Below left   The Crown Range Road goes ever on as it descends from 1119.7 m. The highest through-road in New Zealand, it was so named by the pioneers W.G. Rees and Nicholas von Tunzelmann when they were exploring the area in 1850. It is said that when they saw Lake Wakatipu from the lofty heights, they described their journey as crowned with success. From this vantage point the village of Arrowtown can be seen under the shade of the hills in the distance.

Below right   Autumn mist swirls around the golden tussock-clothed hills at Mt Nicholas, Lake Wakatipu.

JE SUIS L'IMMACULÉE CONCEPTION

Left   The gardens of St Joseph's Church at Jerusalem. A short drive from the Maori pa at Koroniti (Corinth) brings you to this church and the remarkable story of Suzanne Aubert and the congregation of the Sisters of Compassion that she founded in 1892. When I stand here I can feel the annals of time reach out to me palpably — it sends shivers up my spine.

Opposite above   Hunter's Garden Marlborough is one of New Zealand's top garden events. Sponsored by Hunter's Wines, it is a wonderful opportunity to visit some of the best gardens in the country. The gardens may be inspiring, but so are the owners. To visit Devon Gardens was an absolute treat. There is a sheer profusion of colour that spills from all sides, assailing the senses with a heady mixture of perfume that calms the soul as you walk from garden room to garden room. I struck up a conversation with Jill Rogerson who has spent the last ten years developing this wondrous space, and immediately knew that I needed her in my image. Jill is at one with her garden, and her passion has been passed on to it.

Opposite below   The new leaves of silver birches start to reach over this walkway at Larnach Castle on the Otago Peninsula. Below, daffodils welcome the warming sun.

The 'winterless north' is a magnet for holiday-makers from New Zealand and around the world. The benign climate with especially mild winters makes a great escape for those living in the frigidity of the south. Here at Kerikeri, the largest growing town in Northland, there are also a number of history lessons available. It was here in 1819 that the Maori first welcomed missionaries to New Zealand, and also where the first grapevines were planted. The historic Stone Store across from the inlet is the oldest building in New Zealand.

I first visited Whangaroa Harbour in 2004 and could immediately see why this area is renowned for its water activities. The land around the harbour is slowly being encroached on by the ever-expanding lifestyle-block movement that is prevalent in this country at the moment, so I am pleased I saw it before humanity took over the trees. Many of the boats seen here are used for big game fishing, the sheltered harbour providing a perfect refuge before the boats move out into the Pacific Ocean. In the early 1900s the area was a timber town, where the wanton felling of kauri for profit was what made this part of the country rich.

Left The North American P-51D Mustang is one of the most famous fighters of the Second World War. Developed by the Americans for the RAF, it achieved limited success with the Allison engine power plant. Then an English test pilot suggested replacing the Allison with a Merlin engine which had a two-stage, two-speed supercharger. All of a sudden the Americans had a war winner. It was the first fighter that could escort the American bombers from their bases in England all the way to Berlin, due partly to the revolutionary laminar-flow wing which gave much better fuel efficiency.

Below left The North American Harvard was used as an advanced trainer by the RNZAF from 1941 until 1977. Upon retirement, a number were purchased by ex-RNZAF pilots and syndicated to save costs, and thus was born the New Zealand Warbirds Association (NZWA). Captain John Lamont, a retired Air New Zealand pilot, flew the type in the RNZAF and has been involved with the NZWA since its inception. Now actively retired in Wanaka, he flies a number of warbirds, including the Lavochkin La-9, Curtiss Kittyhawk and, of course, the Harvard. It was in one of these aircraft that I flew my first aerobatic sortie and this allowed me to perfect the art of flying upside down and taking photos at the same time!

Below right The Yanks! I photographed this amazing formation over Lake Hawea in 2005. From front to back we have a Boeing Stearman (piloted by Brendan Thow), a North American Harvard (piloted by John Lamont) and a Curtiss P-40 Kittyhawk (piloted by Ray Hanna). This line-up represents the three phases of an American pilot's journey to become a fighter pilot — from basic to advanced trainer and then on to the nimble P-40. The RNZAF operated over 200 P-40s in the Second World War, and this is the only airworthy example extant that flew with the RNZAF. For this photo she appears in the colour scheme of the American Flying Tigers. Unfortunately the photograph can never be repeated. Ray Hanna died of a heart attack in late 2005 and the collection was then split up and sold.

Above Kaikoura offers all that is good about our country: calm seas, verdant green fields, snowcapped mountains and dramatic skies. Add to this the wonderful crayfish that abound on this coast and it becomes a place to satisfy all needs.

Right New Zealander Phil Keoghan is known around the world as the presenter of the Emmy award-winning show *The Amazing Race*. In 2005 I had the pleasure of working with him on a series covering filming locations in New Zealand. Phil has a very quick wit, total sense of adventure and 100 per cent enthusiasm for everything, so this ensured I had a great time. Standing on a cliff top on the side of Mt Earnslaw near Glenorchy — it seemed the perfect place to photograph him. Although he has travelled the world, Phil has a love of his home country and the scenery that abounds here.

Waitukei is a bronze sculpture in the Government Gardens in Rotorua. Created by Rotorua artist Lyonel Grant, it was unveiled in 2001 to mark the new millennium. It is inspired by the melding of Maori and European cultures.

The drive from the city of Wanganui to the small settlement of Pipiriki alongside the Whanganui River must be classified as one of the best road trips in the world. The scenery is fantastic, but more than anything it is the mix of two cultures that is most evident. The river was the main source of transportation for both the original Maori and the European settlers who arrived to 'educate' and convert the natives. Here in the village of Koroniti (Corinth), the local marae welcomes all to enter and be at peace.

Tucked away in an unremarkable industrial area of Petone is an absolute treasure. Stansborough Fibres has a story to tell that is unique in this country. Barry and Cheryl Eldridge purchased Stansborough Farm over 12 years ago after moving from England in 1971. They discovered a breed of rare grey sheep called the Gotland Pelt. It took over 10 years to create the special wool breed of unique grey sheep known as the 'Stansborough Grey' and now they are the only examples of their kind in the world. The 'Stansborough Grey' wool is spun and then woven at the Stansborough Weaving Mill in Wellington. The looms at the mill date from the early 1890s and are two of only four left in Australasia. They are among the first mechanical looms ever designed and are capable of fine or chunky weaves, small or large commercial runs. The mill is open to the public and is an absolute treat to visit. These operating looms are something that you just have to see, and the sound is unbelievable — twice now I have stood spellbound as the looms start working and a deafening racket fills the room. My mind immediately runs back in time when whole factories of these looms were producing fabric. The Industrial Revolution might have changed the face of the world, but what did it mean for the many thousands of workers who had to work in absolute bedlam, seven days a week, for a pittance? Barry and Cheryl are remarkable people and I really enjoy their company. Barry has such an empathy with this equipment — I just had to take a portrait of him as he explained the workings of these archaic monsters to a visiting tour group.

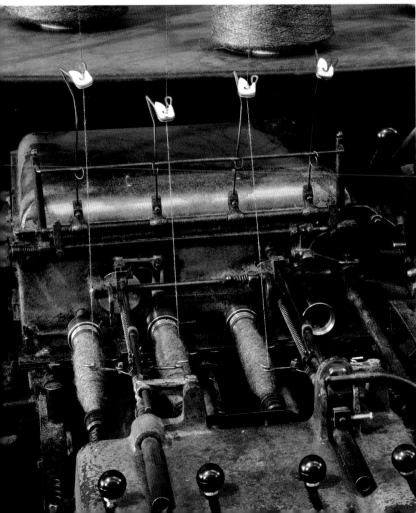

I first travelled along this road in 2005 — I should have done it earlier. Although you can travel from Wanganui on the coast to Raetihi in National Park in about three hours, allow at least a full day to explore. The interplay of water, trees and sunlight beckoned me to stop every two minutes as around every corner a new scene unfolded.

The sun pours through a break in the trees on the bushwalk to view Okere Falls near Rotorua.

Opposite above   Nowhere else in the country can you find such interesting rock shapes so close to the sea than at Kaikoura. Wind has eroded away their softer underbelly and left this starkness that seems at one with the sea and the sky.

Opposite below   The colour of the sea is so evident here near Kaikoura as kelp is washed in the eddying flow of the tide and the moss weed growth on the rocks counterpoints the deep colour of the sea.

Right above   One evening in Kaikoura when the sea was calm, I ventured to the south side of the peninsula to capture the water. When it is almost dark you can set your camera up for exposures of up to 30 seconds and here you can see the results: the gentle breathing of the sea is muted into a flat roll.

Right centre and below   The golden colour of kelp in the blue Pacific Ocean near Kaikoura.

Above   The colours of Southland always seem to include green. A wet spring with good growth and abundant sunshine provided this scene which captured my attention near Winton. The sheep and their offspring look very happy with life!

Opposite above   I distinctly remember my first drive through the Homer Tunnel. Travelling with my parents on our first South Island holiday, we were absolutely amazed at the sheer weight of mountains that tower down as you approach the tunnel. It can be quite daunting as this huge rock wall appears to block all further access, and then the tunnel mouth appears. My mother was not happy at all at the thought of descending into this hole, and it was only the cajoling of the rest of us that finally swayed her.

Opposite below   What a great name for a restaurant. Despite the negative-sounding connotations, the Rat & Roach in Lyttelton is very popular with the locals and serves a very mean burger. The township here has changed over the years, and has moved from a bit of a rough-and-ready port town to a trendy café scene with some great places to eat and a vibrant farmers' market.

Left I remember these types of fuel bowser as a child, when my Uncle Bud used to take me to Boron in Otahuhu. These are real pumps — none of those push-buttons for me. The dial seemed to go around a lot slower then too.

Opposite The town of Cromwell grew in the halcyon mining days of the nineteenth century. The destruction of the Cromwell Gorge and drowning of this historic town to create power was needed, but is still mourned by me and many others. Old Cromwell Town is now a collection of galleries, boutiques and cafés — a far cry from what these stores would have sold a hundred years ago. The wheels serve as a reminder of those days when it was a harrowing bone-jangling ride to the fields of gold from the port city of Dunedin.

The village of Albert Town is situated 7 km from Lake Wanaka. Incredible growth over the last ten years has seen the village spread from its base beside the banks of the Clutha River to the surrounding flatlands. Clear water and excellent fly fishing at Deans Bank (centre right) ensure the camping ground (front) is a very popular spot with summer holiday-makers. Until the single-lane bridge was built in the late 1800s, a ferry stood on the banks of the Clutha to carry people across the swiftly flowing river.

The golden boughs of autumn signal the dramatic change of seasons in Central Otago near the Clutha River at Albert Town.

Above I must admit I have a fascination with cemeteries. The sombreness combined with the lives of people no longer with us and the touching words of a tombstone hold my attention. Most cemeteries also have areas set aside for our armed forces, and often tell sorry stories of our heroes. Here at the Eastern Cemetery in Invercargill these two graves drew my attention. Obviously these two men served their country in the Great War and returned safely home. Why then, five years later did they lose their lives? Injuries, stress, gas? All are possibilities.

Left One of the most thought-provoking and sombre places to visit in Rotorua is Muruika Cemetery, which adjoins St Faith's Church at Ohinemutu. Here, old soldiers are at peace overlooking their lake with the tranquil sounds of the lapping of water and hissing of steam to keep them company. Many of those buried here are from 28 Maori Battalion, who fought with great valour and tenacity during the Second World War. They also paid a high price: over 3500 joined the Battalion and 655 died with a further 1949 being wounded or taken prisoner. This carving standing guard over his flock is known as He Poa.

Opposite Cremation is rapidly becoming the preferred method of burial in this country, and although I realise it is logical I mourn this, as I love to visit cemeteries. To me, the splendid edifices erected to recall families after death just seem to have dignity and create remembrance. These statues tell stories in their solemnity, and their brief words and names spark the mind to wonder who this family was. What were their loves and hates? Which were their happy days? Who were their friends? A grave creates a multitude of emotions that a small plaque will never produce. This single point of remembrance in Eastern Cemetery in Invercargill tells a life story covering many generations. I wonder who they were.

The very appropriately named Smash Palace sits beside SH1 at Horopito. Claimed to be the largest car wrecker's yard in the southern hemisphere, every car known to man seems to reside here in some form of disrepair. Wandering the narrow lanes that separate the vehicles, you cannot help but wonder what story they have to tell. Some like this Thames are victims of old age, while others sit with doors cut off, airbags blown and the tell-tale signs that a tragedy has happened. Car enthusiasts travel from around the world to this Nirvana of automobiles. Somewhere out there is the vital part to return a beloved 'work in progress' to the road.

Opposite and above　The people of New Plymouth have a love affair with gardens, and this is especially apparent in Pukekura Park. Opened in 1876, it is now one of the best inner-city parks in New Zealand. This waterfall in the park always makes me smile. The rocks barely show a glisten of water until the appropriate button is pushed, and then a veritable cascade of water rushes down on command. It might not be completely natural, but the perfectly created steps provide the right flow of misty water. The New Zealand natives on each side complete the scene.

The Remarkables, a range of mountains that look down upon Lake Wakatipu, are aptly named. One of only two mountain ranges in the world that are oriented exactly north to south, it is the serrated tips reaching to a height of 2342 m that provide the perfect backdrop to an alpine resort. Lake Wakatipu was the major transportation route in this area during the gold rush of the late 1800s. At its peak, about 30 boats plied the lake, including four steamers that were brought overland from Dunedin or built on the lakeshore.

I am not one to bungy jump and cannot understand why anybody would want to jump off a bridge with a rubber band around their ankles. The Skippers Canyon Bridge is still an operational bungy drop with a height of 71 m. I'd rather look at it from a helicopter!

I am not a fan of swimming and in fact I would have to say I have never been above my waist in the ocean. This aversion to drowning doesn't mean that you can't enjoy the surroundings, however. Mt Maunganui was a playground 30 years ago, and it has grown to a city many times its size when I knew it. Luckily, the beach remains the same, and the rock pools, surf and soft sand still beckon to both young and old.

Right   I first discovered the Coromandel Peninsula as a teenager, spending many weekends there in a VW Kombi van. The sea and bush meet on golden sands to provide some of the best beaches in New Zealand, with some fantastic fishing along the coast. Here at Timaru Bay north of Coromandel the sea-going escapades are definitely tide related, and give an indication of the tidal reach of the sea.

Below left   Until a few years ago, land in the Catlins was a bargain. Buying a nice tract and setting up a crib was achievable for many people. Now, land prices have rocketed and large modern homes fill many spaces. I love photographing these cribs, and though there may not be a soul around, the laughter of children, the chink of bottle tops and the crackle of a barbecue are embedded in their walls, as loud as ever.

Below right   Situated 25 km from Alexandra, the delightfully named Ophir has had a varying population over the years. Visiting the town now is like stepping back in time to a New Zealand of 50 years ago. It's no wonder that it has been used in two feature films of that era. After gold was discovered in 1863, the name was changed in 1875 from Blacks to Ophir, in honour of the biblical land where the Queen of Sheba obtained gold for King Solomon. As the gold declined, so did the population from its peak of 1000 to less than 50. Today an increasing number of people visit the town as they bike or walk the Central Otago Rail Trail. There are many historically protected buildings in the town with the Post Office a classic, but I just love the 'old town' feel of The Old Drapery Shop.

Lake Wanaka is another jewel in the Southern Lakes crown. One of the best ways to see the lake and its tentacle arms that probe right to the feet of the mountains is by aeroplane. The striking peak of Mt Aspiring can be seen middle left and from this angle you can easily see why it has been dubbed the Matterhorn of the South. Reaching 3033 m high, it was first climbed in 1909. The Maori call her Tititea, which translates as 'glistening peak'. A gravel road can take you over 30 km up the Matukituki Valley (left of Mt Aspiring) and there are some excellent tramps to the foot of Tititea herself.

Lake Hawea has a grandeur that its more popular cousin, Lake Wanaka, will never possess. The shape of the lake and the mountains that perfectly encircle it are nothing short of magnificent. On a perfectly still night I often sit and watch as the sun sinks behind me, leaving just a margin of light that reveals the razor-sharp mountains in perfect clarity.

Above The wine industry is now a huge part of the Marlborough economy. One can drive for miles on end with the company of grapevines on each side of the road.

Left The pinot grape is now synonymous with Central Otago wine, and some excellent pinot noir wines are produced in the area. The combination of large diurnal temperature variations with hot summers and long cool autumns works with the clay terroir to provide a special micro-climate that exists only in three parts of New Zealand, Oregon in the USA and Burgundy in France. Here at Mt Difficulty at Bannockburn, the vintners have been producing superb pinot since 1998. The quality of wine brings chefs from all over the world.

Opposite below The Waihopai Valley near Blenheim is one of contradictions. Home to many vineyards, the vines at one place have strange companions. Home to a New Zealand government tracking station, the radomes have mixed with the grapes to create the very appropriately named Spy Valley vineyards. The fertile, free-draining stony soils are the result of successive flood events and glacial outwash deposits over the previous 10,000 years, and the varietals produced here are outstanding. My vote is for the merlot.

Opposite   Native to North America, the California poppy (*Eschscholzia californica*)
brightens many roadsides in the South Island. Considered by many to be a weed because
of its rampant growth, I think we could find a lot worse weed varieties. Certainly in
Marlborough the type makes a welcome cover, and provides a very colourful counterpoint
to the deep-blue skies and green vines that are a signature of the landscape.

Above   *Papaver orientalis*, Seymour Square, Blenheim.

The Clock Tower in Hastings' Central Mall was completed in 1935 to restore a working clock chime to the city centre after the earthquake. Art deco in style, it is really quite modern in its simplicity and clarity of form.

The Gilray Fountain on Napier's foreshore looks as if it was created in the 1930s. In fact, it was completed in the 1970s using a bequest left by the late Thomas Gilray OBE.

Sunrise over Lake Wakatipu from Mt Nicholas. As the sun rose over The Remarkables in the distance, a warm glow enveloped the hills in the foreground. No wonder photographers call that hour of sunrise the magic hour.

Left Dinghy — Otago Peninsula. The city of Dunedin is justifiably called the 'Edinburgh of the South'. It is not just the city that should claim this accolade, however. A drive around the Otago Peninsula with its bays and hills is very similar to travelling around the southern highlands of Scotland.

Below left Fur seals bask in the sun near Kaikoura. The New Zealand fur seal (*Arctocephalus forsteri*) is endemic to this country, the sub-Antarctic islands and the south coast of Australia. They settled in the Kaikoura region in the 1980s, and there are now approximately 2000 in the area. There are several quite large colonies that can be viewed from the road, and I can spend many hours watching them as they frolic around the rocks and bask in the sun. They may seem ungainly on land, but I would never put myself between one and the sea. The momentum of a 200 kg male is not something I wish to experience.

Below right I consider the swan to be one of the most elegant birds that inhabit this planet. Their symmetry in flight is equalled by their gracefulness on the water, and there is always the beauty of the water as it reacts to their presence.

Opposite above and below   A spring sunset illuminates grapes at Ata Rangi Estate near Martinborough. Meaning 'new beginning' or 'dawn sky', this area was a barren five-hectare paddock when Clive Paton bought it in 1980. He was one of a handful of winemaking pioneers in Martinborough, then a forgotten rural settlement, who were attracted to the area by three key features — the localised, free-draining shingle terrace some 20 m deep; the lowest rainfall of anywhere in the North Island; and the proximity to the capital city of Wellington, just an hour away.

Right above   Poppies and vines together at Ata Rangi Estate Vineyard.

Right below   Lavender sparkles in the sun at Ata Rangi Estate.

As a child I lived in Auckland, and every summer holiday we travelled somewhere exciting. Having relatives in the Manawatu meant that we often traversed SH1 via Taupo. A soon as the plumes of the Wairakei geothermal power station were spied from the back seat, I knew the next stop for my parents to have a 'cuppa' was the Huka Falls. From the small car park, the river was not even visible, but the roar of water gave away the secret of the falls. It is not their height that is impressive, but the sheer flood of water, as the Waikato River plunges over the 11-metre drop at around 220,000 litres per second.

The thundering Okere Falls have also echoed to the thunder of war over the years. The Okere River is also known as the Kaituna (from the Maori 'kai' meaning food, and 'tuna' meaning eels) and is indeed a rich source of food, gifting eels, whitebait and koura (freshwater crayfish) to whomever wishes to take it. Over many centuries, warring Maori tribes have clashed over its ownership. Today the aquatic bounty remains, but the clash of clubs has been replaced with the splash of oars and shrieks of tourists as whitewater rafters brave the highest (7 m) commercially rafted waterfall in the world.

Above This railway goods shed was immortalised by the magnificent artwork of Grahame Sydney. I cannot even attempt to follow his genius, but every time I pass through Wedderburn on that part of SH85 known as The Pigroot, I pause to remember this great artist's work.

Opposite I classify this long drop as one of the best in the country. It sits high atop the Raggedy Range at Poolburn, and I do feel it does need a window. To sit in this high place in quiet contemplation before being whisked away by helicopter on further adventures is a happening not to be missed.

A spring morning near Blenheim as the vines show their first signs of growth and the warming sun dispels any thoughts of winter.

The magnificent view of Hawke's Bay from atop Te Mata Peak. The peak rises 399 m above sea level, and on a fine day you can see right across to the ski slopes of Mt Ruapehu. In summer the brown tussock of the area shows the debilitating effect of the hot northwesterly winds that predominate. As the mercury reaches the low 30s, the shimmering grass is a delight to behold.

From Pipiriki, the Whanganui River road climbs away from the river and bush into more ordered farmland. From the top of one ridge, the three peaks of Ruapehu, Tongariro and Ngauruhoe in the Tongariro National Park can be seen in the distance.

Opposite   The West Coast of the South Island erupts with colour in the spring. In Central Otago, on the other side of the Southern Alps, the lowly buttercup is non-existent, but here it flourishes in great swathes of colour.

Above   I first met the woodland *Trillium* when we lived in Christchurch and immediately fell in love with its simple beauty. Hailing from North America and Asia, the type is on the endangered list in both countries. Here it flourishes in the woodland gardens of Larnach Castle on the Otago Peninsula.

Left White Island (or Whakaari as it was named by the Maori before Europeans arrived) lies 48 km off New Zealand's Bay of Plenty coastline and is accessible by boat or helicopter from the mainland. An active volcano, it is often called the vent for the thermal area of Rotorua. Sulphur used to be mined here until an eruption killed a number of workers. As well as the sights and sounds of an active volcano, I enjoyed seeing the magnificent gannet colonies that abound away from the main crater. We chose the luxurious way to see the island, cruising past on a Crystal Cruises liner with a latte in hand.

Below left If you want a real holiday, there is nothing better than cruising. I have been very fortunate in spending time with Crystal Cruises aboard their ship, the *Crystal Serenity*, on her voyages around New Zealand as I discuss film tourism. I just call this image 'The Art of Cruising'.

Below right Tauranga Bay is a surfer's delight (not that I like surfing in any form). The sight of the sea crashing onto the shore does enthuse me, however, and here, near the very appropriately named Cape Foulwind, the sea always appears the most amazing green as the wind whips the waves. Nearby Westport is a great little town that has some wonderful restaurants and bars, and just a short drive away are these wonderful beaches. Tauranga Bay features a number of surf carnivals during the year, and the best place from which to watch these is the Tauranga Bay Café with its great food and good coffee.

Above I drive through this scene frequently, as it is only 15 minutes from home, but I never tire of the way the trees change colour and the snow advances and recedes, or how the sky changes hue. This view is now forever called The Great East Road: it was in the middle-distant trees that the Flight to the Ford was filmed in *The Fellowship of the Ring*.

Left Mt Nicholas Station runs over 27,000 merino sheep for the fine wool they produce. Ability to withstand drought and cold make these sheep ideal in this part of the world. The ultra-fine quality of their wool is becoming world renowned, in part due to the new woollen products from the Icebreaker brand, which was born in Queenstown.

Above   Situated halfway through the Kawarau Gorge between Cromwell and Queenstown, Roaring Meg is a well-signposted and popular stop for tourists. Most stand and admire the original power station firing its water into the gorge and then continue on their journey. If only they would cross the road into the reserve, because here water is being channelled in the way nature designed. Roaring Meg is born high in the ranges that divide the gorge and the Cardrona Valley Road. For the energetic there is a great one-day walk that will take you between the two points. As for me, I am happy to sit in this beautiful reserve and admire nature's falls.

Opposite   The town of Cromwell, situated at the confluence of the mighty Clutha and Kawarau Rivers, has undergone many changes since I first visited in 1970. Half the town has been flooded to make way for power generation, and the population has quadrupled. However, some of its charm still remains at Old Cromwell Town, a road and old buildings that slope down to the all-devouring river. On most Sundays, a farmers' market takes up residence, selling the best produce, meat and flowers that Central Otago can offer. If you are passing through, it is well worth a stop.

Right   Wide-flowing rivers are a feature of the West Coast landscape. The narrow strip of land between the sea and the Southern Alps provides many contrasts as the bush gives way to fertile farmlands, but always the high peaks stand in the background. Another feature of these rivers is the annual run of whitebait from the sea. Caught in the lower reaches of the rivers, whitebait (or inanga) are individually only 25–30 mm in length. They are eaten completely, most commonly as a whitebait fritter, where egg whites are mixed with the small fish to create a subtle patty, where nothing can take away the flavour of the fish.

Below left   The local pub at Blackball has an interesting history. In 1928 this small locale on the West Coast had a population of over 1200, all working the area's coal mines. All were thirsty no doubt, and the pub saw its fair share of parties and brawls, and in the way discussions happen in pubs, it also saw the birth of the New Zealand Labour Party. The closure of the mines in the 1960s saw the hamlet shrink in size, and other than a small explosion of hippies who arrived to grow herbs, the town was expected to die. But a good town never dies, and now some of the best salami in the country comes from Blackball, and once again visitors stay at the pub. The hotel's name, The Dominion, was changed to The Hilton to honour the mine manager, not the hotel chain. The hotel chain was not amused, however, and legal proceedings followed. Now it is simply called 'Formerly The Blackball Hilton'.

Below right   Real estate for sale in the commercial centre of Blackball.

Left and oppopsite The Wintergardens are a classical feature of the Auckland Domain. Developed after the First World War, they are now a protected heritage site. The renaissance-style central pond with appropriate statues is a popular place to relax, but the two large hot-houses hold the real treasures. As a child I was taken into these warm moist habitats by my flower-loving parents and what a treasure trove was revealed inside. As the water dripped off the roof, the humid air was rich with the aromas of a thousand plants, all with complicated names that my parents seemed to know. I returned in 2006 after an absence of 35 years and nothing seemed to have changed. The aroma instantly brought back a thousand memories of childhood.

Visitors travelling south from Dunedin to Invercargill have a choice of two routes. I am not decrying SH1 but I would certainly recommend the journey via the Catlins. It is an area of majestic seascapes, waterfalls, and native flora and fauna that make the journey worthy of at least a two-day sortie. On my first visit to Purakanui Bay I chanced upon a strong southwest storm that seemed to be blowing straight from Antarctica. Between the stinging showers of bitterly cold rain, the sun would momentarily appear to bathe the sand in a warm glow and illuminate the grass. I marvel at this southern rata tree here. It seems to be able to withstand any force thrown at it — it's a little thin around the edges but has a good strong bushy top.

Right The view from the top of Deer Park Heights is astounding. Lake Wakatipu seems to stretch to infinity, while the golden tussock-covered peaks provide a perfect backdrop. I prefer visiting this area when a nor'west wind is slowly starting to blow. The tussock shimmers in the strengthening breeze and clouds form as the heat rises over the mountains. If you could ever tire of looking at this combination, you could cast your eyes in other directions and see the many exotic animals that graze the slopes. You may spy a bison that looks slightly familiar — it was the model for the mythical Warg that appeared in *The Lord of the Rings* as created by the art department at Weta Workshop.

Below left Earnslaw Burn may not be a well-known locale for many Kiwis, but it has been seen all around the world. A favourite for television commercial directors, it has seen skydivers descend upon it, and Jeeps and other assorted objects have been extolled from its valley. The towering Mt Earnslaw, reaching 2819 m, was used in *The Lord of the Rings* film trilogy.

Below right In 1999 a visit by a location scout changed the lives of the Alexander family at Matamata for ever. Within a year, a part of their farm had become the most famous address in Middle earth. This cohesive family has worked incredibly hard to retain this little piece of the Shire and to turn it into a well-run tourist attraction. The sets were never built to last, however, and in 2005 the original Bag End was consigned to the wood pile and a more permanent example was put in place. What Sauron failed to achieve, the Alexander family did in a week.

Above and opposite   The New Zealand Gardens Trust has designated Barewood Gardens in the Awatere Valley a 'garden of national significance', and rightly so. The large house features sweeping verandas that invite you to pause and sip a cold drink as the hot Marlborough sun beats down. Around every corner is another delight and, for me, a love of potagers and honeysuckle ensured that this image had to be placed in the book. In one small corner, this alcove caught my eye — the perfectly situated urn gives a Mediterranean feel to an otherwise very English setting. The garden is normally open to visit and is also one of the stops during the Hunter's Garden Marlborough festival.

Ummm . . . which way was that again? Signs at Coromandel.